CANADA'S MULTICULTURAL SOCIETY TODAY

Weigl

Published by Weigl Educational Publishers Limited
6325 10 Street SE
Calgary, Alberta, Canada
T2H 2Z9

Website: www.weigl.ca
Copyright ©2012 Weigl Educational Publishers Limited
All rights reserved. No part of this publication may be reproduced, stored in a retrieval system,
or transmitted in any form or by any means, electronic, mechanical, photocopying, recording,
or otherwise, without the prior written permission of the publisher.

Library and Archives Canada Cataloguing in Publication data available upon request.
Fax 403-233-7769 for the attention of the Publishing Records department.

ISBN 978-1-77071-706-0 (hard cover)
ISBN 978-1-77071-709-1 (soft cover)

Printed in the United States of America in North Mankato, Minnesota
1 2 3 4 5 6 7 8 9 0 15 14 13 12 11

072011
WEP040711

Photograph Credits
Every reasonable effort has been made to trace ownership and to obtain permission to reprint copyright
material. The publishers would be pleased to have any errors or omissions brought to their attention so
that they may be corrected in subsequent printings.

Weigl acknowledges Getty Images as its primary image supplier for this title.

Project Coordinator: Aaron Carr
Art Director: Terry Paulhus

We acknowledge the financial support of the Government of Canada through the Canada Book Fund
for our publishing activities.

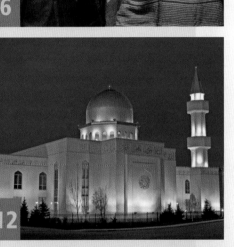

Contents

One Country, Many Peoples 4

Community Festivals 6

What is Multiculturalism? 8

Case Study: Multiculturalism in Calgary 10

How do Canadians Feel About Multiculturalism?..............12

How Racism Develops 14

Case Study: The Girl in the Hall 16

Canada's Changing Aboriginal Communities 18

Case Study: The Dene Declaration 20

The Creation of Nunavut 22

Achieving Workplace Fairness 24

What is Your Viewpoint? 26

Learn More About Canada's Multicultural Society 28

Testing What You Have Learned 29

Skill Builders 30

Glossary 31

Index 32

Opening ceremonies at the 2010 Winter Olympic Games in Vancouver, British Columbia, included a celebration of Canada's Aboriginal traditions.

One Country, Many Peoples

Imagine a photograph so large that it includes every single Canadian citizen. Such a photograph would include people who are as different as the many countries from which they came. They would have their own ideas about education, business, health, marriage, family, and religion.

These ideas would be as diverse as the peoples' backgrounds. All, however, are part of the Canadian community. Canada's peoples share more than the same location on the globe. They share a common desire to create the best way of life possible for themselves and their communities.

When they take the Oath of Citizenship, newcomers pledge to observe the laws of Canada and fulfill their duties as Canadian citizens.

Most Canadians regard themselves as part of different types of communities at the same time. For example, someone may live on a street in a particular neighbourhood, but that neighbourhood is part of a larger town or city, which is part of a province or territory, which is part of Canada. Depending on the circumstances, people may identify themselves as belonging to one or more of these communities.

Each person contributes to a community in an individual way. In equal societies, all citizens enjoy the same opportunity to participate in community life. At various times, a community may help, teach, guide, and support its members. In return, each individual member has a responsibility to give something back to the community.

While all Canadians belong to Canadian society, each person belongs to other groups as well. Each Canadian participates in a number of different activities. These activities bring people with a variety of **values**, beliefs, and behaviours together in groups. Each group is a kind of community, with common interests or bonds. For example, people who are members of the same club may follow certain rules of behaviour or a special dress code. Members of a religious group are expected to uphold certain beliefs and ways of behaving. Each group influences its members in distinctive ways and helps to define who they are.

Making Choices

Some people say Canadian society should be a melting pot, in which **immigrants** blend into the mainstream culture. Others say Canada should be a mosaic, in which differences between cultures are valued and preserved. In a recent survey of more than 1,000 Canadian adults, 54 percent said Canada should be a melting pot, while 34 percent favoured the idea of a mosaic. Which do you prefer? Why?

Community Festivals

Many Canadian groups preserve their distinctive cultural traditions though community festivals. In Alberta, for example, people celebrate their Western traditions with events like the Calgary Stampede and the Heritage Festival in Edmonton. Multiple events at the Head-Smashed-In Buffalo Jump Interpretive Centre, a World Heritage Site near Fort Macleod, commemorate Aboriginal hunting traditions. Dance competitions, arts and crafts, and other activities celebrate the Aboriginal Peoples' traditional way of life.

In many cities across Canada, Chinese communities put on parades during their New Year's festivities in January or February. Colourful dragons and ceremonial dances fill the streets. Many Chinese traditions are observed at this time. A New Year's banquet is a time for the whole family to get together to feast on a wide variety of special dishes. Dessert is usually a New Year's cake that is round and made from sweet, sticky rice. The shape of the cake symbolizes completeness, while the sweetness expresses the hope for a sweet new year.

Somalis are among more than 80 peoples represented at the annual Heritage Festival in Edmonton, Alberta. Thousands of Somali refugees came to Canada in the early 1990s.

Fish is served because, to the Chinese, it means abundance or plenty. Traditionally, the fish is prepared whole, with head and tail intact. By serving fish at the New Year's banquet, family members express their hopes for food, money, health, and happiness in the year to come.

Christmas and Hanukkah are examples of community festivals based on religious events. Christmas traditions include attending worship services, decorating the Christmas tree with bright lights, giving gifts to friends and relatives, and gathering for a large festive dinner. During Hanukkah, also known as the Festival of Lights, Jews light candles in a **menorah** over a period of eight days. To celebrate Hanukkah, Jewish families typically exchange gifts and dine on potato pancakes known as latkes.

Different festivals in the Atlantic provinces recognize and celebrate the rich cultural heritage of this Canadian region. The Annapolis Valley Apple Blossom Festival, for example, focusses on the agricultural heritage of Nova Scotia, while the Loyalist City Festival in Saint John, New Brunswick, pays tribute to the **United Empire Loyalists** who settled that province. Perhaps the best-known **Maritime** celebration is the Lucy Maud Montgomery Festival in Cavendish, Prince Edward Island. This festival of island life and culture honours the works of Lucy Maud Montgomery, author of the *Anne of Green Gables* stories.

Think About It

Think about festivals celebrated by your family or by other people in your community. What are some different kinds of celebrations in which you participate?

More than 400,000 Chinese live in and around Vancouver, British Columbia. The city hosts one of Canada's largest Chinese New Year parades.

Green Gables House on Prince Edward Island commemorates the life and works of Lucy Maud Montgomery.

What is Multiculturalism?

Canada is a country of new beginnings. Many people originally came to Canada to start new lives. Some were fleeing oppression, others sought cheap land, and still more wanted an opportunity to get ahead. Whatever their reasons for coming, all of these immigrants thought that Canada offered them a better way of life.

In the past, Canada relied on immigrants to fill its vast spaces and develop its many resources. Today, the Canadian government continues to welcome newcomers. More than 2.4 million immigrants arrived in Canada between 2000 and 2010. More than 40 percent of the population living in the Toronto **metropolitan area** is foreign-born. Population experts have predicted that by 2031, nearly one-third of all Canadians will belong to a **visible minority** group. Examples of visible minority groups include Chinese, Indians, Pakistanis, Arabs, Filipinos, and Koreans.

Canada is often described as a multicultural country. This means that Canada consists of diverse cultures existing side by side in the same place or region. Examples of the nation's cultural diversity can be seen in almost any Canadian city. Typically, a delicatessen selling mostly smoked meats from Germany might stand next to restaurants specializing in British fish and chips, pizza and pastas from Italy, or sushi and other delicacies from Japan. Down the street might be an Aboriginal Friendship Centre or a Hungarian community hall.

With more than 100,000 new immigrants arriving every year, Toronto, Ontario, is one of the world's most diverse cities.

The federal government forecasts that metropolitan Montreal's visible minority population will grow from 604,000 in 2006 to more than 1.5 million by 2031. Montreal is home to Canada's largest Arab community, including many Arab immigrants from North Africa who continue to press for greater democracy in their home countries.

Some parts of the city, such as Chinatown, might have street signs in different languages. Churches, synagogues, mosques, and temples devoted to many different religions can also be found.

Canada's multicultural society might be compared to a large symphony orchestra. A large orchestra consists of many different instruments. The violins, brass, woodwinds, keyboards, and drums look and sound completely different from each other.

How do they make beautiful music together? First, the players must master their own instruments. They must practise until they can play their instruments as well as possible. Then they must master the art of playing together as a group.

They do this by listening to, learning from, and respecting each other.

Multiculturalism in Canada works in a similar way. There is great diversity between the different communities, just as there is great diversity between the different sections of the orchestra. Nevertheless, each section has an important part to play. When communities are willing to co-operate, the result is harmony rather than discord.

Think About It

Students, teachers, and school administrators all come from different groups and perform different tasks. What kinds of attitudes and behaviours can help make your school an interesting and effective place to learn?

Case Study | Multiculturalism in Calgary

An ethnically and culturally diverse population offers many advantages to communities. Many immigrants bring a strong work ethic with them when they come to Canada, and they do not take their jobs for granted. Many also bring savings that they invest or use to start businesses of their own. This contributes to a healthy local economy.

One example of a Canadian city that has benefited from its ethnically diverse population is Calgary, Alberta. Various Aboriginal groups have lived in the Calgary area for at least 12,000 years.

The fur trade brought Europeans into the region. American bison hunters and whisky traders built forts, one of which was located at the present site of Calgary. Settlement of the region brought the North-West Mounted Police to the area to keep the peace and stop the whisky trade. They built Fort Calgary in 1876. In 1883, the Canadian Pacific Railway arrived, bringing immigrants from all over the world.

Today, the city of Calgary is home to more than 1 million people. More than one-fifth of all current Calgary residents were born in countries other than Canada

Held in July, the Calgary Stampede attracts more than 1 million visitors each year.

A centre for the global energy industry, Calgary is one of Canada's fastest-growing cities.

Among the members of more than 200 ethnic groups that live in the Calgary region are people of British, German, Irish, French, Ukrainian, Chinese, Indian, Polish, Dutch, Scandinavian, Italian, Russian, and Aboriginal backgrounds.

Calgary's metropolitan area population grew by about one-third between 1999 and 2009. Immigrants account for most of Calgary's population growth. Many of the new immigrants to Calgary are young adults. As a result, the city's average age is well below the national average.

Calgary's future success will depend on its ability to attract and maintain a young, well-educated, and diverse population.

Canada's major cities have mosques where Muslims worship. Today, Muslims represent one of the fastest-growing religious communities in the country.

How do Canadians Feel About Multiculturalism?

Many studies in recent years have attempted to find out what Canadians think about multiculturalism. In one recent survey, more than 1,000 Canadians were asked whether they thought multiculturalism had been good or bad for Canada. The results showed that about 55 percent of Canadians thought multiculturalism was good or very good for the country, 30 percent thought it was bad or very bad, and the remainder were not sure. About 68 percent of Canadians between the ages of 18 and 34 thought multiculturalism was good or very good, compared with 45 percent of those over 65.

Earlier, a survey team interviewed 2,000 Canadians concerning their feelings about their country. People were read a list of statements about Canada and were asked to rate them on a scale of 0 to 10 based on whether or not the statements made them feel proud to be Canadian. The researchers defined responses from 0 to 2 as "not at all proud," from 3 to 7 as "neutral," and from 8 to 10 as "very proud." Here are some statements along with the responses the researchers received.

- The vastness and beauty of the land: 88 percent very proud, 11 percent neutral, 1 percent not at all proud.
- The fact that people from different cultural groups in Canada get along and live in peace: 70 percent very proud, 27 percent neutral, 3 percent not at all proud.

Young people tend to have a more positive view of multiculturalism than do older Canadians, according to the most recent Statistics Canada surveys.

- Multiculturalism: 54 percent very proud, 37 percent neutral, 8 percent not at all proud.
- Having two official languages, English and French: 41 percent very proud, 38 percent neutral, 21 percent not at all proud.

Support for multiculturalism in this survey was particularly strong among immigrants. Nearly two-thirds of the immigrants said that multiculturalism made them feel very proud to live in Canada. Among non-immigrants, only 52 percent showed similar enthusiasm.

In general, most Canadians believe that diversity enriches Canadian culture. They believe someone can be a loyal Canadian while at the same time remaining proud of a distinct cultural heritage. On the other

hand, some Canadians worry that Canada cannot maintain a strong national identity if members of all the different cultural communities hold on to their distinct cultural identities. These Canadians believe that multiculturalism divides instead of unites.

One area of concern has been the treatment received by certain visible minority groups. By law, every Canadian has the same rights and privileges. In daily life, however, people sometimes receive unfair treatment because of negative **stereotypes** held by others. This form of prejudice is called **racism**.

Think About It

What makes you feel most proud to be a Canadian? Are there any ways you think life in Canada could be improved?

How Racism Develops

Until laws and attitudes changed in the 1950s and 1960s, Black people in the American South were required to use separate drinking fountains.

Prejudice or discrimination against people of a particular race or ethnic background is called racism. Groups that are targets of racism are often not allowed to participate fully in society because of the prejudice against them. A well-known example of racism is the way many white Americans used to treat Blacks. In the South, African Americans were not allowed to mingle with whites. Blacks and whites were required to attend separate schools and could not eat in the same restaurants. When they travelled on buses, African Americans had to sit in the back. The laws did not change until civil rights leaders such as Martin Luther King Jr. challenged them in the 1950s and 1960s.

Racism sometimes flares up when new immigrants arrive. Every year, for example, Canada grants permanent resident status to about 250,000 immigrants. There are legitimate arguments to be made both for and against accepting this many newcomers. Many people feel that Canada's economy and society cannot absorb so many new people at once. Others argue the opposite, contending that immigrants contribute much more to the country than they cost.

Attitudes toward immigrants may harden into prejudice when people see competition from newcomers as the main cause of economic and social problems.

people have trouble finding jobs, for example, they may blame their problems on the newcomers who speak, behave, and worship in ways that are different from the mainstream culture. These newcomers may also be singled out because of their skin colour or style of dress.

Some forms of racism can be dealt with by laws that protect people from racist behaviour. It is illegal, for example, to refuse to rent an apartment to someone because of that person's skin colour. Most provinces have **human rights commissions** to deal with complaints of discrimination and racism.

Laws and commissions are not the only answer. Some forms of racism are so subtle that laws cannot deal with them. Sometimes people are even guilty of racism without realizing it. The real key to ending racism and discrimination is to learn to treat all people with respect and dignity. Canadian schools, cities, community groups, clubs, and hospitals participate each year on March 21st in the International Day for the Elimination of Racial Discrimination.

Although Sikhs have often been targets of prejudice in Canada, their numbers have continued to increase. Today, about half of all Canadian Sikhs live in British Columbia, where they make up about 3 percent of the total population.

Making Choices

Imagine you are with a group of people eating lunch. You hear racist comments being made about a classmate. How would you respond?

Some Canadians have been active in opposing racism and religious prejudice.

Case Study | The Girl in the Hall

Danielle Gallant, a 13-year-old student at St. Stephen's High School, Stephenville, Newfoundland, wrote this story based on her own experience. Danielle questioned her actions after witnessing an example of discrimination in her school.

It was on a morning in November when I saw for the first time the new girl with the olive complexion and curly black hair. She wore a long flowered skirt and an obviously very aged white blouse. She crept slowly down the hall with an air of uncertain hesitation about her. As she walked, she kept her back against the hard tiles of the wall as if she wanted to remain as inconspicuous, as unnoticeable, as she could. With each step a small, brown foot peeped out from under her skirt and

I could see that all she wore on her feet were a pair of worn leather sandals.

I could tell that she was new to our town, this girl with the strange clothes, because when she approached a teacher and spoke to him, the words were not familiar to me. The few recognizable words she did speak were thick and slurred. The teacher did not understand. I could see that right away, and the girl sank back towards the locker with an embarrassed look on her face.

Suddenly, a loud giggle pierced the air. A few lockers away, a group of people had formed. It was easy to see that they were laughing at the new girl. I looked her way to see if she had noticed, but she just turned away.

In a survey sponsored by the Association for Canadian Studies and the Canadian Race Relations Foundation, 50 percent of people between the ages of 18 and 24 said they had witnessed a racist incident in the past year.

Gradually, a group of students gathered round the girl. By now, the first bell had rung and the girl was clearly confused. No one seemed to notice or care. All they noticed was that dark skin, those big black eyes, and those funny clothes.

The crowd became bolder and bolder. The muffled giggles grew into outright laughter and now there wasn't an eye in the hall that wasn't focussed on the unfortunate girl.

I looked away. I couldn't stand to see her face. I couldn't look at her, knowing how much she must be hurting. I wanted to help her, wanted to stand up for her. More than anything, I wanted to tell these people how wrong they were, how cruel they were being. I wanted to make them feel as badly as she must have been feeling.

Instead, I just stood there. I was scared to say anything. Scared that these people would tease and laugh at me, just as they teased and laughed at her.

Finally I forced myself to look at her face. Written there I saw all the pain and anger I knew I would see, but there was something else, something I hadn't expected. Her expression revealed a clearly defined look of acceptance as if she had expected this, and had decided that she must put up with it. I knew then that none of this was new to her; she had seen it all before. The whispering, the laughter, the teasing, it was all the same to her.

Voices began to rise out of the crowd. I could hear the jokes, the insults, and I knew she could too. I glanced over at her and saw that despite the fact that she spoke a different language, she understood what they were saying. There were some things that run deeper than words. They are part of an international language, understood by all people, no matter who, no matter where.

The second bell rang and the hall cleared. Only the girl and I remained. Suddenly she turned and I found myself looking into sparkling black eyes that were overflowing with tears. I shivered, conscious of the uncanny feeling that this girl with her penetrating gaze knew what I was thinking.

A feeling of guilt washed over me. I'd had the chance to help this girl. I could have been a friend when she needed one. But I hadn't. I had done nothing.

I turned away and began to walk down the hall. I told myself that it wasn't my fault and that it wasn't my responsibility to stick up for her. But somehow, I couldn't remove the feeling that I had, in some way, treated her just as the others had. I was as bad as they were.

I glanced over my shoulder, only to see her still standing there. She looked at me and I could tell she wanted my help. I turned away and walked down the hall. I didn't look back.

Making Choices

Danielle's story is about one person's feelings after seeing someone ridiculed for being different. The fact that Danielle felt uncomfortable and unhappy about what happened shows that she is beginning to rethink her behaviour. How might Danielle have acted differently? What could the girl in the hall do to stop this type of treatment by her classmates? Write another ending to Danielle's story, or write about a similar incident from your own experience.

Annual gatherings such as the Kamloopa Pow Wow in Kamloops, British Columbia, have helped to preserve First Nations traditions.

Canada's Changing Aboriginal Communities

Aboriginal Peoples make up an important part of Canada's multicultural society. These groups have undergone major changes in recent decades. Between 1986 and 2006, for example, the number of people describing themselves as **Métis** increased by 278 percent. During the same period, the **First Nations** population jumped by 109 percent, and the Inuit population rose by 68 percent. All three figures far exceeded Canada's population growth rate of 25 percent during the same 20 years.

Three reasons account for the rapid increase in Aboriginal population. First, Aboriginal groups have higher birth rates than other Canadians. Second, census takers have been doing a better job of identifying and counting Canada's Aboriginal Peoples. Third, and most important, when asked which group they belong to, more Canadians have been choosing to identify themselves as Aboriginals. This change marks a turning point in the history of Canada's Aboriginal groups.

The arrival of European colonists in the early 17th century opened a difficult chapter in the history of the Aboriginal Peoples. The European settlers tried to impose their own way of doing things.

As a result, Canada's First Peoples suffered many hardships. The Aboriginal groups accepted some of the new ways, but they refused to give up all of their own traditions, or to surrender their separate identity.

In recent decades, Canada's Aboriginal communities have found new strength in their traditional ways. Aboriginal leaders, such as Harold Cardinal, Elijah Harper, Ovide Mercredi, and Sheila Watt-Cloutier, have spoken out for Aboriginal rights. Many Aboriginal groups desire to take more responsibility for their affairs and to rely less on federal and provincial governments. Aboriginal Peoples want more control of their own education, health, and legal systems. This process is known as self-government.

By 2010, 17 self-government agreements involving 27 communities had been completed. Often, these agreements accompanied other agreements that settled land disputes between Aboriginal groups and the federal, provincial, and territorial governments. Nearly 400 other Aboriginal communities are seeking their own self-government agreements.

Aboriginal communities have begun the process of creating their own laws, police forces, and education and justice systems. In time, many Aboriginal groups hope to achieve **self-determination**, which is the right to make their own choices about their future instead of having everything decided for them by government.

Born in northern Quebec, Sheila Watt-Cloutier has been an Inuit activist for more than two decades. She has represented the Inuit in conferences dealing with the impact of global climate change on Arctic peoples. She was nominated for a Nobel Peace Prize in 2007.

Think About It

Why have increasing numbers of Canadians chosen to identify themselves as members of Aboriginal groups? What does this say about the status of Aboriginal groups within Canadian society?

Case Study | The Dene Declaration

Fewer than 45,000 people live in the Northwest Territories, which covers an area of almost 1.2 million square kilometres. Aboriginal Peoples, including the Dene, Métis, and Inuit, account for about half the total population of this rugged land.

The Dene are one of Canada's First Nations. Their name means "people" in the Athapascan language. In 1970, the Dene established the Indian Brotherhood of the Northwest Territories, or N.W.T. Five years later, the Indian Brotherhood issued an important statement of Aboriginal rights. This statement is known as the Dene Declaration. The Indian Brotherhood represented both the Dene, who had **treaty** *rights, and the Métis, who did not. Although the Indian Brotherhood no longer exists, both these Aboriginal Peoples are now represented by the Dene Nation.*

We the Dene of the N.W.T. insist on the right to be regarded by ourselves and the world as a Nation.

Our struggle is for the recognition of the Dene Nation by the Government and the people of Canada and the peoples and governments of the world.

As once Europe was the exclusive homeland of the European peoples, Africa the exclusive homeland of the African peoples, the **New World**, North and South America, was the exclusive homeland of Aboriginal peoples of the New World, the **Amerindian** and the Inuit.

The New World like other parts of the world has suffered the experience of **colonialism** and **imperialism**. Other peoples who have occupied the land—often with force—and foreign governments have imposed themselves on our people. Ancient civilizations and ways of life have been destroyed.

Colonialism and imperialism are now dead or dying. Recent years have witnessed the birth of new nations or rebirth of old nations out of the ashes of colonialism.

As Europe is the place where you will find European governments for European peoples, now also will you find in Africa and Asia the existence of African and Asian countries with African and Asian governments for the African and Asian peoples.

The African and Asian peoples—the peoples of the Third World—have fought for and won the right to self-determination, the right to recognition as distinct peoples and the recognition of themselves as nations.

But in the New World the Native Peoples have not fared so well. Even in countries in South America where the Native Peoples are the vast majority of the population there is not one country which has an Amerindian government for the Amerindian peoples.

Nowhere in the New World have the Native Peoples won the right of self-determination and the right to recognition by the world as a distinct people and as nations.

While the Native People of Canada are a minority in their homeland, the Native People of the N.W.T., the Dene and the Inuit, are a majority of the population of the N.W.T.

The Dene find themselves as part of a country. That country is Canada. But the Government of Canada is not the government of the Dene. The government of the N.W.T. is not the government of the Dene. These governments were not the choice of the Dene, they were imposed on the Dene.

What we the Dene are struggling for is the recognition of the Dene Nation by the governments and peoples of the world.

And while there are realities we are forced to submit to, such as the existence of a country called Canada, we insist on the right to self-determination as a distinct people and the recognition of the Dene Nation.

We the Dene are part of the Fourth World. And as the peoples and nations of the world have come to recognize the existence and right of those peoples who make up the Third World, the day must come and will come when the nations of the Fourth World will come to be recognized and respected. The challenge to the Dene and the world is to find the way for the recognition of the Dene Nation.

Our plea to the world is to help us in our struggle to find a place in the world community where we can exercise our right to self-determination as a distinct people and as a Nation.

What we seek then is independence and self-determination within the country of Canada. This is what we mean when we call for a just land settlement for the Dene Nation.

Unanimously passed, Joint National Assembly, Fort Simpson, 1975.

In recent years, First Nations and their American Indian allies have continued to protest what they call unfair treatment of Aboriginal Peoples by the Government of Canada.

Think About It

What rights were the Dene people demanding? To what extent have these demands been met?

Iqaluit, the capital of Nunavut, has a population of more than 7,200.

The Creation of Nunavut

The most important change on the map of Canada in 50 years took place on April 1, 1999. On that date, the new territory of Nunavut was established. The territory is now home to more than 33,000 people, most of whom are Inuit. The Inuit have lived in this area for thousands of years. Nunavut means "Our Land" in Inuktitut, the Inuit language.

The creation of Nunavut followed years of talks between the Inuit and the Canadian government. In 1990, land claims settlements were reached with the Inuit and with the Dene and Métis of the Northwest Territories. Two years later, residents of the Northwest Territories approved the idea of dividing the region, with the eastern portion becoming Nunavut. In May 1993, Canadian Prime Minister Brian Mulroney went to the small village of Iqaluit on the shores of Frobisher Bay on Baffin Island. There, he signed an agreement giving the Inuit control of a territory larger than the three Maritime provinces combined.

Singing, drumming, and dancing accompanied the ceremonies to mark the establishment of Nunavut in 1999. Jean Chrétien, who had followed Mulroney as prime minister, described the day as one "of great joy for me, for Nunavut and for Canada." Paul Okalik, the 34-year-old lawyer who became the territory's first premier, said: "We the people of Nunavut have regained control of our own destiny."

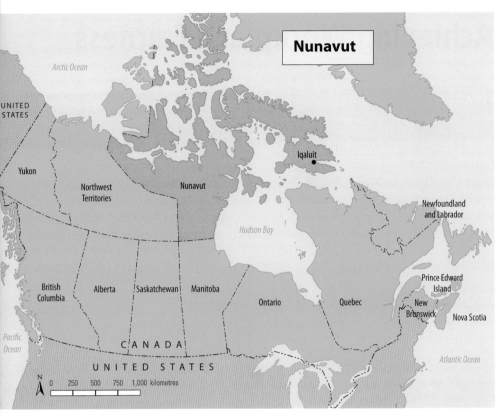

Nunavut is both the youngest and the largest of Canada's provinces and territories. It covers more than 2 million square kilometres and accounts for more than one-fifth of Canada's total land area.

Nunavut's flag, adopted in 1999, features an Inukshuk, a traditional stone monument. The Inuit and other Arctic peoples use a stone Inukshuk to mark travel routes, fishing and hunting grounds, and sacred places.

Achieving Workplace Fairness

In order for a multicultural society to succeed, all groups must feel that they are being treated fairly. Employment is one area where fairness is essential. In the early 1980s, it became clear that some Canadians seeking good jobs were not being treated fairly. A commission was appointed to find out what steps the government could take to remove barriers to hiring and promotion. The commission's ideas became part of the Employment Equity Act. This federal law was passed in 1986 and revised in 1995.

Employment equity is a government program that attempts to make sure that jobs are open to all qualified people, regardless of their gender, skin colour, physical disability, racial background, or religious beliefs. It removes barriers so that more women, Aboriginal Peoples, people with disabilities, and visible minorities can enter the work force or can get promotions in their jobs. One way the government can enforce this law is to withhold money from companies that violate it.

Canada's visible minority population is expected to increase from 5.3 million in 2006 to between 11.4 million and 14.4 million by 2031.

The program does more than punish companies that fail to comply. The program also singles out firms that take positive steps to promote diversity. A recent government report praised the National Bank of Canada, which has more than 13,000 employees and is the leading bank in Quebec. The company sponsored a diversity week that included a wheelchair basketball game, an African-inspired Teranga festival, and a dinner at a restaurant where meals were served in the dark by staff with serious visual problems. Many employees and managers participated in these and other events. They showed the company's employees and the wider community that the bank valued diversity and was open to meeting the different needs of different groups.

Many organizations receive money from the federal government. When the government required them to start employment equity programs, some organizations introduced these programs just to avoid losing their government money. Employment equity programs are still controversial. Some people claim that they are a form of "reverse discrimination." These critics mean that, instead of making everyone equal, employment equity makes it more difficult for people not included in the special groups to find jobs. They worry that employers who are encouraged to hire more women, Aboriginal Peoples, people with disabilities, and visible minorities will overlook other qualified people who do not fit into any of these categories.

Defenders of employment equity argue that the program aims at equal treatment, not preferred treatment. They say that by removing the barriers that some people face, the program allows all qualified

Wheelchair curling was a medal event at the Paralympic Games for athletes with disabilities, hosted by Vancouver in 2010. People with disabilities are protected under the Employment Equity Act.

people an equal opportunity to find work. "The way I see it, diversity isn't just a buzzword, it's a fundamental value," said Louis Vachon, the president of the National Bank of Canada. "I want it to become an integral part of our culture and for all of us to make promoting it part of our daily mission."

What is Your Viewpoint?

Diversity is part of everyday life. Large numbers of Canadians live in communities with people of different cultural backgrounds. These communities change over tim as they adapt to changing circumstances. Sometimes changes happen on their own. At other times, they are shaped by new laws and regulations.

For more than a quarter century, the Canadian government has had laws requiring employment equity programs that improve access to jobs and promotions for women, Aboriginal Peoples, people with disabilities, and visible minorities. Do you agree with this approach?

Viewpoint #1
We don't need the government telling companies who to hire. Employers should have the right and the ability to choose the best person for the job.

Viewpoint #2
Some people would not have jobs if the government did not have programs like employment equity. These programs remove barriers.

Viewpoint #3

These laws only affect companies that do business with the government. I think the law needs to go further. Discrimination by anyone against any group should be illegal. If we're going to be a multicultural country, we should practice what we preach.

Viewpoint #4

I want to be judged on my abilities and my suitability for a job, not on my gender or cultural background.

Viewpoint #5

Employment equity programs lessen my chance of getting a job because I am not a member of the target groups. This is reverse discrimination. I think it's unfair.

Learn More About Canada's Multicultural Society

1. Would you describe your community as culturally diverse? Explain, using examples. Consult census reports in your local library or online. Does this additional research confirm your earlier impression? Has your community become more diverse or less diverse since 2001?

2. As a class, write to the Chamber of Commerce or Tourism Office in cities and towns across Canada to find out about interesting festivals in their communities. Much of this information can also be found online. On a classroom wall or school website, create a calendar of community events and festivals. What do these festivals indicate about Canada's cultural heritage and diversity?

3. Brainstorm a list of all the people you know. Make the list as long as you can. After you have completed the list, begin to group the names into common categories. These categories might include relatives, classmates, team or club members, people you see on the weekend, the friends you skateboard with, and so on. Place these groups of names into circles. Each circle represents a different community of people. To how many communities do you belong?

4. Nunavut has existed for more than a decade. Find out as much as you can about Canada's newest territory. How has self-government changed the lives of the people who live there?

Q List at least two traditional ways of celebrating the Chinese New Year.

A The Chinese celebrate New Year's Day with a parade featuring colourful dragons and ceremonial dances. A New Year's banquet usually includes fish served whole and a round cake made from sweet, sticky rice.

Q Who was Lucy Maud Montgomery? Which Canadian province holds a festival named after her?

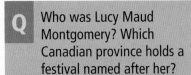

A Lucy Maud Montgomery is the author of the *Anne of Green Gables* series. She was born on Prince Edward Island, which each year holds a festival in her honour.

Q What single factor most accounts for Calgary's rapid population growth?

A Immigration has been the most important contributor to Calgary's rapid increase in population. More than 20 percent of Calgary residents are foreign-born.

Q The story "The Girl in the Hall" shows the effects of:
(a) self-determination
(b) racism
(c) reverse discrimination
(d) immigration

A (b) Racism. The other students hold negative stereotypes about her based on her skin colour and clothing.

Q True or False: Canada's Aboriginal population has been declining since the 1980s.

A False. Canada's Aboriginal population has increased much more rapidly than the nation as a whole.

Q Name Canada's newest territory. When did it come into being? What is its main population group?

A Nunavut, Canada's newest territory, became a reality in 1999. The Inuit make up Nunavut's main population group.

Skill Builders

1. In 2010, Angus Reid Public Opinion asked more than 1,000 Canadians the following question: Overall, would you say Canada is a **tolerant** or **intolerant** society toward each of these groups? The survey then listed a series of minority groups. Look at some of the results in the table and then answer the questions below.

	TOLERANT	INTOLERANT	NOT SURE
Muslims	52%	33%	15%
Aboriginal Canadians	62%	30%	9%
Immigrants from South Asia, such as India and Pakistan	64%	24%	12%
Immigrants from Africa	72%	16%	12%
Immigrants from Asia, such as China and Hong Kong	81%	10%	9%
Immigrants from Latin American countries	79%	7%	14%
Immigrants from Europe	89%	4%	7%

Some percentages do not add to 100 because of rounding.

- Toward which group did people think Canada showed most tolerance?

- Toward which group did people think Canada showed least tolerance?

- If the same question had been asked 100 years ago, do you think the results would have been different? How?

- How can Canadians do a better job of treating all people with tolerance and respect?

2. Create a mosaic or scrapbook showing as many of Canada's different peoples as possible. Illustrate your project with original artwork or with colourful clippings from magazines, newspapers, or Internet printouts.

3. Create a description for a job of your choice. Role-play an interview with someone applying for the job. Be sure to ask fair questions that are sensitive to a person's cultural background. At the same time, the interview should be useful in finding out whether or not the applicant has the right skills for the job.

4. In 1870, the Métis drew up a List of Rights. Find out as much as you can about the Métis and about the List of Rights they sent to the Canadian government in Ottawa. Compare the Métis List of Rights with the Dene Declaration issued in 1975. In what ways are they similar? In what ways do they differ?

Glossary

Amerindian: the original inhabitants of the western hemisphere south of the Arctic coastal regions

colonialism: the idea that one nation has the right to claim and control other nations as its colonies

employment equity: a government program that attempts to remove barriers to hiring and promotion for women, Aboriginal Peoples, people with disabilities, and visible minorities

First Nations: a term used collectively to describe Canada's Aboriginal Peoples, with the exception of Métis and Inuit

human rights commissions: government agencies that act to protect people and groups against discrimination in employment, housing, and other areas of public life

immigrants: people from one country or region who come to live in another

imperialism: the idea that a powerful country has the right to form an empire that dominates other nations and takes their resources

intolerant: the opposite of tolerant

Maritime: name given to a region on Canada's east coast, including the provinces of New Brunswick, Nova Scotia, and Prince Edward Island

menorah: the candle holder used by Jews in celebrating the festival of Hannukah

Métis: a Canadian people who trace their origins to the marriage of Europeans with Aboriginal Peoples

metropolitan area: a large city and its surrounding suburbs

New World: the western hemisphere, especially as it appeared to European explorers and colonists

racism: discrimination or prejudice against a person or group based on racial, ethnic, or cultural differences

self-determination: the right of a community or nation to make its own decisions, without having those choices dictated by another nation or government

stereotypes: oversimplified ideas, attitudes, or images applied to all members of a group

tolerant: showing respect to other people's culture, values, and beliefs

treaty: legal agreement negotiated between two or more nations

United Empire Loyalists: American colonists who stayed loyal to Britain after the war that led to the establishment of the independent United States

values: beliefs and ways of doing things that are considered important, either by an individual or by an entire culture

visible minority: as defined by law, someone who is neither Aboriginal nor Caucasian in origin and who is non-white in colour

Index

Aboriginal Peoples 4, 6, 8, 10, 11, 18, 19, 20, 21, 24, 25, 26, 29, 30
Alberta 6, 10
Anne of Green Gables 7, 29

Calgary 10, 11, 29
Calgary Stampede 6, 10
Cardinal, Harold 19
Chinese New Year 7, 29
Chrétien, Jean 22
Christmas 7
colonialism 20

Dene 20, 21, 22, 30

Edmonton 6
employment equity 24, 25, 26, 27

Gallant, Danielle 16

Hanukkah 7
Harper, Elijah 19
Head-Smashed-In Buffalo Jump 6
human rights commissions 15

immigrants 5, 8, 9, 10, 11, 13, 14, 30
imperialism 20
Indian Brotherhood of the Northwest Territories 20
International Day for the Elimination of Racial Discrimination 15
Inuit 18, 19, 20, 21, 22, 23
Iqaluit 22

Jews 7

King, Martin Luther, Jr. 14

Mercredi, Ovide 19
Métis 18, 20, 22, 30
Montgomery, Lucy Maud 7, 29
Montreal 9
Mulroney, Brian 22
Muslims 12, 30

National Bank of Canada 25
New Brunswick 7
Newfoundland 16
North-West Mounted Police 10
Northwest Territories 20, 22
Nova Scotia 7
Nunavut 22, 23, 28, 29

Prince Edward Island 7, 29

racism 13, 14, 15, 29
"reverse discrimination" 25, 27, 29

self-determination 19, 21, 29
self-government 19, 28

Toronto 8

United Empire Loyalists 7

Vachon, Louis 25
Vancouver 4, 7, 25
visible minorities 8, 9, 13, 24, 25, 26

Watt-Cloutier, Sheila 19